A Young Girl's Dream

A YOUNG GIRL'S DREAM

CARLA ANNE ARNESON

With gratitude, I would like to thank

The girls who helped create the photographs
for *A Young Girl's Dream*

The women who dreamed, dared,
and led the way for all of us

Marie C. Wilson, founder of The White House Project

Johnnie Hyde, Raven Productions, for her
belief in *A Young Girl's Dream*

. . . .

Printed in Canada at Friesens
First Printing: 2018
22 21 20 19 18   5 4 3 2 1

Cover and page design by Mayfly Design and typeset in the Futura and Stone Sans typefaces

Library of Congress Cataloging-in-Publication Data
Names: Arneson, Carla Anne, 1950-
Title: A young girl's dream / by Carla Anne Arneson.
Identifiers: LCCN 2011038075 | ISBN 9780983518914 (hardcover : alk. paper)
Subjects: LCSH: Self-esteem in women. | Women—Biography.
Classification: LCC BF697.5.S46 A76 2018 | DDC 155.5/33—dc23
LC record available at https://lccn.loc.gov/2011038075

Raven Productions, Inc.   Ely, Minnesota

Dedicated to my mother, Dorothy, who dreamed with me.
An artist, she taught me to see.

Who knows when the dream begins . . .

A young girl dreamed she would ski to the South Pole.

Someone said she was not strong enough.

She did not believe it.

A young girl dreamed she would achieve justice.

Someone said she expected too much.

She thought the world did not expect enough.

A young girl dreamed she would run like the wind.

Someone said it was impossible.

She knew impossible was just a word.

A young girl dreamed she would be an artist.

Someone said it was a foolish dream.

She did not believe it.

A young girl dreamed she would be a figure skater.

Someone said nothing mattered but winning gold.

She thought doing her best mattered more.

A young girl dreamed she would be an astronaut.

Someone said she dreamed too big.

She knew no dream was too big.

A young girl dreamed she would be a police officer.

Someone said it was too difficult for a woman.

She did not believe it.

A young girl dreamed she would be a journalist.

Someone said it could be dangerous.

She thought truth was worth the risk.

A young girl dreamed she would be a scientist.

Someone said men are better scientists than women.

She thought that was silly.

A young girl dreamed she would change her world.

Someone said she was not smart enough.

She did not believe it.

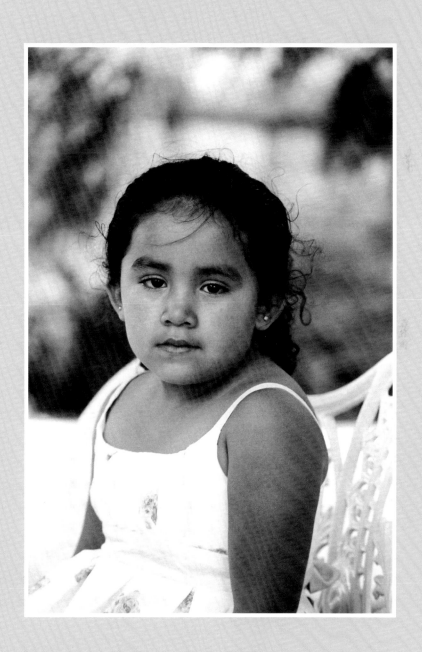

A young girl dreamed she would be a great singer.

Someone said she could not perform in her own country.

She sang anyway.

A young girl dreamed she would dance for the world.

Someone said she was too shy.

She kept dancing.

A young girl dreamed she would be a homemaker.

Someone said that was not a career.

She did not believe it.

A young girl dreamed she would vote someday.

Someone said women would never be able to vote.

She said, "I will."

A young girl dreamed she would be president.

Someone said she should not even try.

She did not believe it.

A young girl dreamed.

No one said she could not do what she dreamed.

No one said she could not be what she dreamed.

Someone said, "Do it."

She believed.

What is your dream?

Believe in yourself and follow it.

The world is waiting.

Women dreamers who changed the world...

Ann Bancroft and Norwegian Liv Arnesen were the first women to ski across Antarctica (2001). They received corporate sponsorship for that expedition. But when Ann was planning an earlier expedition to ski from the edge of Antarctica to the South Pole (1993), she could not find sponsors to provide equipment and financial support. In one meeting, a potential sponsor squeezed Ann's biceps and said, "You aren't strong enough to pull a 250-pound sled on the harshest continent in the world." Ann led three women on that expedition to the South Pole, supported by grassroots fundraising, and she proved she was strong enough. In 1995, Ann was inducted into the National Women's Hall of Fame. I was inspired to create this book in 2008 when I heard Ann tell her story at The White House Project's political leadership training in Tower, Minnesota.

Winona LaDuke is Anishinaabe, an enrolled member of the White Earth Band of Ojibwe. Winona empowers Native American women, encouraging them to become involved in issues they care about. She is internationally known as a strong voice for indigenous economic and environmental concerns. In 1993, Winona and the Indigo Girls, Amy Ray and Emily Saliers, established Honor the Earth, focusing on environmental justice. In recognition of her leadership and community commitment, Winona was inducted into the National Women's Hall of Fame in 2007.

At the 1960 Summer Olympic Games, Wilma Rudolph became the first woman from the United States to win three gold medals in track and field during a single Olympics. She was called the fastest woman in the world. Her wins were especially remarkable because she had had polio when she was a child and it had been hard for her to even walk. Wilma encouraged others to believe in themselves: "Never underestimate the power of dreams and the influence of the human spirit. We are all the same in this notion. The potential for greatness lives within each of us."

Mary Cassatt (1844–1926) was an Impressionist painter and a printmaker. She found inspiration in the lives of women, particularly the relationship between mothers and children. In spite of her family's initial objections, she became an artist at a time when it was not an acceptable profession for a woman. Mary believed in painting women as subjects not objects. Her artwork now hangs in national and international art museums. Alma Thomas (1891–1978) was an Expressionist painter and art educator. Alma was the first African American woman to have her artwork placed in the permanent collection of the White House. Her painting *Resurrection* was also put on public display by First Lady Michelle Obama and President Barack Obama.

Winner of two Olympic medals, five world championships, and nine U.S. championships in figure skating, Michelle Kwan said in 2015, "You do learn something from sports that's good and true wherever you go, and that's the value of aspiration. In every great thing we try, there are bound to be disappointments and challenges ahead, and I believe aspiration is what carries you through." Regarding disappointments, Michelle told her audience, "The true test, I believe, is how we all recover." After the 1998 Winter Olympic Games, Michelle was saddened by the results, yet when interviewed later, she made the often-quoted statement: "I didn't lose the gold. I won the silver."

Astronaut Dr. Ellen Ochoa was the first Hispanic woman in space (1993). One of her role models was Dr. Sally Ride, the first woman from the United States in space (1983). Ellen is a research engineer and inventor. In 2012, Ellen was the first Hispanic woman, the second woman, to become director of the Johnson Space Center; the first woman was Dr. Carolyn L. Huntoon. Ellen was inducted into the U.S. Astronaut Hall of Fame in 2017. Former NASA astronaut Dr. Mae C. Jemison, engineer and physician, was the first African American woman in space (1992). Mae once said, "Don't let anyone rob you of your imagination, your creativity, or your curiosity. It's your place in the world; it's your life." In 2015, Mae received the Elizabeth Blackwell Award for outstanding contributions to the advancement of women in medicine. Mae is also a dancer and sees the connection between art and science.

Studies have shown that physical strength of police officers does not determine job performance or ability to deal with dangerous situations. Lola Baldwin (1908) and Alice Stebbins

Wells (1910) were thought to be the first policewomen. However, recently discovered documents show Marie Owens was hired by the Chicago Police Department in 1891. Throughout her 32-year career, Marie was dedicated to helping women and children. New York City Police Department Officer Moira Smith died saving others during the terrorist attack on the Twin Towers, September 11, 2001. Moira was the first officer to report the attack, and she is credited with saving hundreds of lives during the evacuation of the South Tower (2 World Trade Center). Moira was posthumously awarded the NYPD Medal of Honor for her heroic actions.

Maria Hinojosa is an Emmy Award–winning correspondent, television anchor, and producer. She finds and reports the untold stories of people too often ignored, giving them a voice. Author Michi Nishiura Weglyn gave Japanese Americans a collective voice when she wrote the investigative book *Years of Infamy: The Untold Story of America's Concentration Camps* (1976). Gwen Ifill was a trailblazing broadcast and print journalist, as well as an author. In 1999, Gwen became the first African American woman to host a major political talk show. Remembering Gwen, President Barack Obama said, "She was an especially powerful role model for young women and girls who admired her integrity, her tenacity, and her intellect." Christiane Amanpour spoke eloquently for the children of Bosnia in her news story "War Through the Eyes of Children" (1992). Marie Colvin, renowned correspondent, was also a voice for the innocent children of war. Just before her death in 2012, Marie reported from Syria, alerting the world to the suffering of the Syrian children.

Elizabeth Blackwell became the first woman to graduate from medical school in the United States. She graduated at the top of her class from New York's Geneva Medical College in 1849. It had been very difficult for her to find a school that would allow a woman to study medicine. In 1889, Susan La Flesche Picotte became the first Native American woman to receive an M.D., graduating as valedictorian from the Woman's Medical College of Pennsylvania, the world's first medical school established for women. Rachel Carson was a zoologist, marine biologist, and author who courageously worked to protect our environment; *Silent Spring* is her best-known book. Rachel was posthumously awarded the Presidential Medal of Freedom in 1980. In Europe, in 1903, Marie Curie became the first woman to win a Nobel Prize (with her husband, Pierre, and Henri Becquerel). Marie was also the first person and the only woman to win two Nobel Prizes: the 1903 Nobel Prize in Physics and the 1911 Nobel Prize in Chemistry. In 1935, Marie and Pierre Curie's daughter Irene (with her husband Frédéric Joliot-Curie) won the Nobel Prize in Chemistry.

Dolores Huerta is a children's activist, a women's activist, and a labor and civil rights activist who cofounded, with Cesar Chavez, the organization that would eventually become the United Farm Workers. Throughout her life, Dolores has worked to protect farm workers and their families. She began one career as a teacher. Then Dolores decided she needed to do even more to help children in her community. Many of the children came to school hungry, making it difficult for them to concentrate. Dolores believed she could make a difference by helping their families achieve better working conditions and wages. In 1993, Dolores was inducted into the National Women's Hall of Fame. In 1998, she received the Eleanor Roosevelt Award for Human Rights from President Bill Clinton. In 2012, President Barack Obama presented her with the Presidential Medal of Freedom.

Marian Anderson was one of the most gifted and famous singers of the twentieth century. In 1939, the Daughters of the American Revolution refused to allow Marian to perform in Constitution Hall because she was black (a decision the group has said it deeply regrets). In response, First Lady Eleanor Roosevelt helped make it possible for Marian to perform on the steps of the Lincoln Memorial in Washington, D.C., to an audience of 75,000 people, and to millions more listening over the radio. One of the songs Marian sang was "My Country, 'Tis of Thee." In 1955, Marian was the first African American soloist to sing with the New York Metropolitan Opera. Marian received the Presidential Medal of Freedom in 1963 and the National Medal of Arts in 1986.

Maria Tallchief was a world-famous ballerina. When she was young, Maria was quiet and reserved, some thought shy. Maria loved to be outdoors. In her autobiography she wrote, "Mostly, I longed to be in the pasture, running around where the horses were." As a dancer, Maria Tallchief dazzled audiences with her athleticism and passion; perhaps her most famous role was in the ballet *Firebird*. Maria was inducted into the National Women's Hall of Fame in 1996 and received the National Medal of Arts in 1999.

Homemakers and mothers have long changed the world. They have supported and encouraged the dreams of children in their care; they have pursued their own dreams. Jane Addams dedicated her life to improving the lives of immigrant families in the United States, particularly women and children. Jane established a home for an entire community, Hull-House, co-founded with Ellen Gates Starr in 1889. Jane had no children of her own, yet through her efforts, generations of children had better educational opportunities and living conditions, as well as protection under the law. Jane was also an outspoken advocate for peace. In 1931, Jane became the second woman—the first from the United States—to win the Nobel Peace Prize (jointly with Nicholas Murray Butler). The first woman to win the Nobel Peace Prize was Austrian Baroness Bertha von Suttner in 1905.

Women did not gain the right to vote in the United States until 1920 with the ratification of the 19th Amendment. Among the women who strove for the right of women to vote were Susan B. Anthony, Elizabeth Cady Stanton, Lucretia Mott, Sojourner Truth, Lucy Stone, Mary Church Terrell, Amelia Bloomer, Frances E. W. Harper, Anna Julia Cooper, Ida B. Wells-Barnett, and Alice Paul. Alice Paul also authored the Equal Rights Amendment, which was first introduced in Congress in 1923. Sojourner Truth, former slave and abolitionist, was noted for her speech "Ain't I a Woman?" given at the 1851 Women's Rights Convention in Akron, Ohio. Harriet Tubman, former slave, abolitionist, and operator of the Underground Railroad, was also a strong supporter of a woman's right to vote. Susan B. Anthony voted on November 5, 1872; she was later arrested and tried for illegal voting. There are still places in the world where women cannot vote.

Throughout history, women have been leaders, sometimes as the first woman elected president of her country. Vigdís Finnbogadóttir was elected president of Iceland in 1980, serving for fifteen years. Mary Robinson was elected president of Ireland in 1990, leading the way for Mary McAleese who was elected Ireland's president in 1997, the first woman in the world to succeed another woman as an elected head of state. Tarja Halonen was elected president of Finland in 2000, reelected in 2006. Ellen Johnson Sirleaf was elected Liberia's president in 2005, making her the first woman in Africa to be a head of state and the first black woman in the world elected president. Ellen was reelected in 2011, the same year she won the Nobel Peace Prize (with Leymah Gbowee and Tawakkol Karman) "for their non-violent struggle for the safety of women and for women's rights to full participation in peace-building work." In the United States, the first woman to run for president was Victoria Woodhull (1872) followed by Belva Ann Lockwood (1884), Margaret Chase

Smith (1964), Shirley Chisholm (1972), Patsy Takemoto Mink (1972), Patricia Schroeder (1988), Carol Moseley Braun (2004), and Hillary Rodham Clinton (2008). They are just a few of the women who have run for president in the United States, yet a woman had not been nominated by either of the top two political parties, Democratic or Republican, until 2016. In 2016, Hillary Rodham Clinton won the Democratic Party's nomination for president of the United States of America.

The year 2020 will be the 100-year anniversary of women having achieved the right to vote in the United States of America.

The presidency is waiting.

"Never doubt that you are valuable and powerful and deserving of every chance and opportunity in the world to pursue and achieve your own dreams."

—Hillary Rodham Clinton